Misery Loves Company

Waterfowling and the Relentless Pursuit of Self-Abuse

Ducks Unlimited, Inc.
Memphis, Tennessee

Text and Photography by Bill Buckley

Ducks Unlimited, Inc.
One Waterfowl Way
Memphis, TN 38120

Text and Photography: Bill Buckley

Book Design: Doug Barnes

Published by Ducks Unlimited, Inc.
John A. Tomke, President
Julius Wall, Chairman of the Board
D. A. (Don) Young, Executive Vice President

ISBN: 1-9617279-8-5
Published September 2002

Printed in Canada

Ducks Unlimited, Inc.
Ducks Unlimited conserves, restores, and manages wetlands and associated habitats for North America's waterfowl. These habitats also benefit other wildlife and people. Since its founding in 1937, DU has raised more than $1.3 billion, which has contributed to the conservation of over 9.4 million acres of prime wildlife habitat in all fifty states, each of the Canadian provinces, and in key areas of Mexico. In the U.S. alone, DU has helped to conserve over 2 million acres of waterfowl habitat. Some 900 species of wildlife live and flourish on DU projects, including many threatened and endangered species.

Library of Congress Cataloging-in-Publication Data

Buckley, Bill, 1958-
Misery loves company : waterfowling and the relentless pursuit of self-abuse / text and photography by Bill Buckley.
p. cm.
ISBN 0-9617279-8-5 (hardcover : alk. paper)
1. Duck shooting--Pictorial works. 2. Goose shooting--Pictorial works. 3. Duck shooting--Humor. 4. Goose shooting--Humor. I. Title.
SK333.D8 B82 2002
799.2'44'0222--dc21
2002012648

Author's Dedication

For Daisy and the Good Doctor: In the immortal words of Mick Jagger, "You can't always get what you want, but if you try sometimes, you just might find, you get what you need..."

Acknowledgments

This book owes everything to the many generous people whose self-deprecating humor, and willingness to be photographed, enabled me to illustrate that a waterfowler's life is not all bright skies and cupped wings. Most of their names have been withheld to protect what's left of their dignity.

Some people, however, were so instrumental to this book that to not mention them would add insult to injury. My special thanks to Coleman Green, for inspiring this book, to the Dixie Farm Hunting Club boys, whose generosity cannot merely be explained by boredom due to the worst hunting season in twenty years (so glad I could share it with y'all!), and to Jay Logsdon, Paul Howard, Chuck Myers, and Robert Powell for tolerating the ever-present camera lens—no small feat.

Finally, I cannot express enough gratitude to John Hayes and Peyton Randolph, whose efforts on my behalf truly made this book possible and exceeded all bounds of friendship. Brothers, you're the best!

Call to Action

The success of Ducks Unlimited hinges upon each member's personal involvement in the conservation of North America's wetlands and waterfowl. You can help Ducks Unlimited meet its conservation goals by volunteering your time, energy, and resources; by participating in our conservation programs; and by encouraging others to do the same. To learn more about how you can make a difference for the ducks, call 1-800-45-DUCKS.

*Thus we see that the lot of the duck hunter
is not a happy one. He is the child of frustration, the collector of
mishap, the victim of misfortune.
He suffers from cold and wet and lack of sleep.
He is punished more often than rewarded.
Yet he continues. Why?*

Ted Trueblood, "This Mania Called Duck Hunting"

*"Man, this stinks!
We haven't seen a duck in two hours."*

*"Make that more like three.
So whaddaya think?
Thirty more minutes?"*

Anonymous Duck Hunters

You can lead a man to frigid water, but you can't make him put on his neoprene and jump in. Only waterfowlers will do that. They gladly leave the comfort of their homes in the predawn black to see out the bleakest marshes and muck-ridden fields where ducks and geese abound. And like sleet driven by a hard north wind, they are unstoppable. Not even the foulest weather or most dangerous commute will deter them.

Contrary to myth, however, waterfowlers are not super-humans who revel in any misery nature blows their way. Truth is, years of smelling swamp gas, wet dogs, and mildewed waders have addled their brains. Wind and cold and severe sleep deprivation have dulled their senses. Bobbing decoys and whistling wings—and no doubt the sour of their own duck calls—have left them spellbound. Never mind the cumulative effect of shooting case after case of 3½-inch shells.

And yet the myth persists. Why? Because it sounds better than the truth.

Of course, compared to upland bird hunters, waterfowlers are a hardy lot. They don't fret about their toes getting cold or their Italian leather shooting gloves getting muddy. They don't mind if a little rain or ice collects on their barrels. Political correctness isn't one of their priorities, so psychobabble like "sadomasochistic," "obsessive-compulsive," and "Don't you think hunting seven weekends in a row is a bit excessive?" rolls off them like water on a greenhead's back. They only care that their buddies are ready to hunt the following weekend. When the Weather Channel predicts gusts up to 25 mph and temperatures in the low 30s, with sleet or snow possible, they'll be heading for the door. So will their friends. Because if misery loves company, tomorrow morning should be one heck of a good time, and no waterfowler in his right mind would dare miss out on it.

*S*o what drives duck and goose hunters, anyway? What makes them abandon warm beds at obscene hours for the discomfort of a distant swamp, pothole, or muddy field?

Frankly, not even they can tell you exactly. But if sometimes they seem a few shells short of a full box, don't think they're clueless. A tired duck hunter is never as dull-witted as he looks.

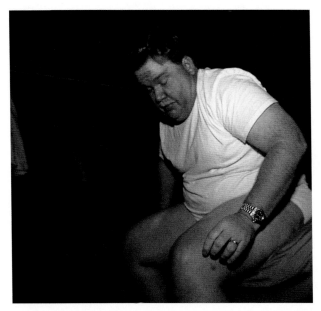

𝓗e knows, for instance, that between superior training and a Lab's natural ability to mark, losing downed birds is never a problem.

And that hunting isn't just about bag limits and killing; part of its appeal is the satisfaction of putting meat on the table, just like our forefathers did.

You might even get a perfect pintail or mallard
mounted, so you can enjoy its beauty forever.

Granted, even the best-trained dog will sometimes do things you'd rather he not . . .

*B*ut to hunt without one inevitably leads to other problems.

In fact, making your own retrieves will quickly bear out a few unpleasant revelations. For example, if you shoot a duck within one hundred yards of a muddy creek, it will surely land not in your spread but on the opposite side.

Speaking of spreads, serious duck hunters diligently keep their decoys, bags, and decoy cords in top working condition.

Why they always end each season with fewer decoys than they started is one of waterfowling's greatest mysteries.

Of course, decoys and trained dogs are pointless if a hunter can't blow a call. So to appeal to the drake or gander's ear, he practices whenever and wherever he can. The next time you see a truck with a DU bumper sticker swerving across traffic lanes ahead of you, don't automatically assume the driver's drunk and then call the police. It might only be the steering wheel slipping off his knees. Goose calling takes two hands, you know.

Although a duck call is a finely tuned musical instrument, non-hunters may not fully appreciate a caller's dedication or skill. But since practice makes perfect, he is forced to continue on, despite the considerable risk of being ostracized by those closest to him.

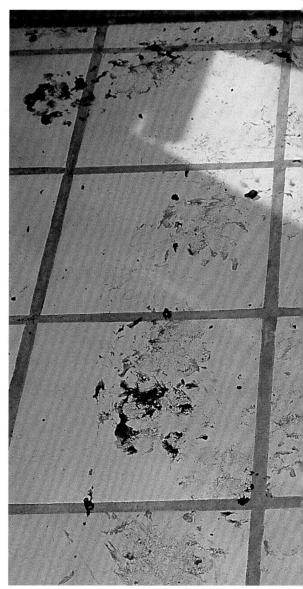

Mind you, at home is nowhere to test your luck. Being careless about where you clean your gun or pluck your geese, or where your retriever goes after a hunt, could affect your hunting plans for the following weekend.

hen again, you can pay now or you can pay later. The experienced waterfowler always lets the bird numbers, and his standing in duck camp, dictate his course of action.

Duck hunters are trained to expect the unexpected and to be self-reliant. Yet sometimes they must rely on the kindness of strangers, no matter how embarrassing the situation.

While his fellow duck hunters also stand ready to assist him through any mishap, their compassion is limited for the ill prepared. Which is why a preseason checkup on your outboard is always wise. They'll tow you to the boat ramp once, maybe twice if the hunting's slow, but start paddling after that. You do have a paddle, don't you?

broken-down motor can mean the difference between suste-
ance and going hungry all morning . . . or going hungry all
ay.

With so many preparations to handle, it's little wonder the waterfowler goes into each season, and each subsequent road trip, a little worse for the wear. Eve Mountain Dew, Nutty Bars, and fried por skins—a balanced breakfast by any hunter's standard—can't keep a man going indefinitely.

*C*atnaps are often the only real rest he'll see from November through January.

ven when he has a real bed to sleep in, there is no rest for the weary in duck camp.

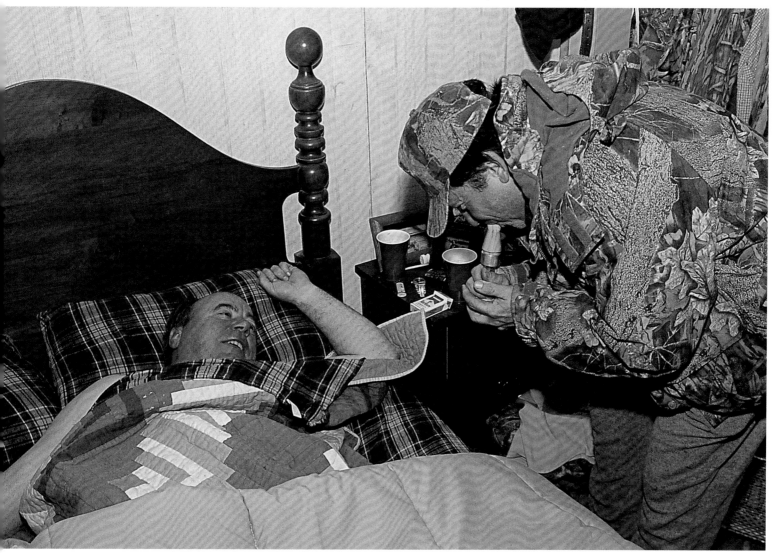

easoned water-
fowlers anticipate
being groggy when
they head out the
door and take the
necessary precau-
tions to ensure
absolutely nothing
gets left behind.
Which is why they
alone account for
90 percent of all
Post-it notepad
sales in North
America.

They understand
that when you
hurry, you're
bound to forget
something.

Of course, even when you think you've allowed enough time to get to the blind by shooting time, it seems like you're always a few decoys shy of being ready for the first flight.

But being on time won't necessarily guarantee you'll connect on the first ducks that fly over. Shoot from a coffin blind and you'll understand why.

Still, a waterfowler's day is ruled by the clock—by one-half hour before sunrise and the exact minute the sun sets—so once he sets out for his blind, his determination knows no bounds. Nothing shall steer him off schedule.

Not the previous week's eleven inches of rain; not the fact that the levy broke and his heavy aluminum boat is now nowhere near water.

*N*o matter how long or difficult the hik or wade in, no matter how treacherous the footing . . .

A waterfowler will always get where he's going, even if he'd rather be somewhere else once he's there . . .

*E*ven if it occurred to him that his special duck hole might freeze up during the minus-20-degree night . . .

Even if his friend's directions to a killer pothole turned out to make no sense.

Because wherever the ducks go, so will the duck hunter. He'll worry about getting back later.

$\mathcal{D}$uck hunters are used to being in sticky situations that challenge their collective knowledge of physics, hydrology, and mechanical engineering. In the rare event even those considerable resources are not enough, it's nice to know there's a tractor nearby.

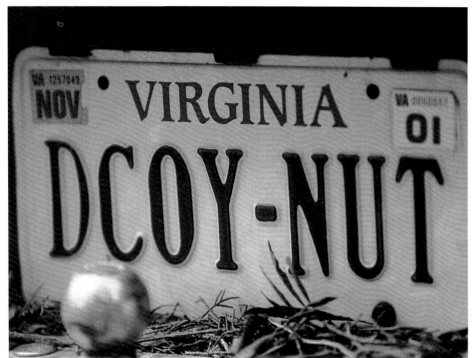

When primitive man conked the first fowl to wander within swinging range of his club and dragged it back to his hut for dinner, he knew he was on to something big. Ever since then waterfowlers have been obsessed with the idea of decoying ducks and geese.

This long and documented love affair with blocks of wood or plastic helps explain a few axioms about hunters and their decoys that will prove true during the upcoming season, just as they did the previous ten.

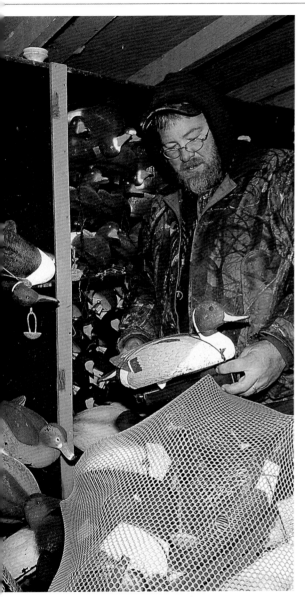

Like the more you take, the better the hunt is bound to be. Forget the fact that the more you set out, the more you have to pick up, and the slower the hunt, the larger your spread will seem.

If you lend your decoys to anyone but your most-trusted hunting partner, you will regret it.

No one will admit to doing it, but some wiseguy will shoot at least one of your decoys this season.

Setting out a spread always takes longer when an excited dog is around.

*E*ven the best-trained dog doesn't know
to swim wide of the decoys.

Motor props and decoy cords do not mix, but if they do, it will happen when you'd least prefer it.

And while you may think you're prepared for any contingency, each time you set out your decoys you'll throw at least one of them an inch or two too far from shore.

henever the ground is frozen rock-
rd and you have to pound holes for the
coy stakes, your partner will spend an
ordinate amount of time setting up his
nd.

*Decoys with multiple parts should be
assembled on shore.*

*A*t least once during the season—due to severe sleep deprivation—your partner will think it's funny splashing you with
decoys. In which case it's perfectly acceptable to reciprocate.

*H*iding your decoy bag so the ducks can't see it will sometimes backfire on you.

Finally, two axioms you will realize time and again: First, even though you rushed to put out your decoys before sunup, the birds will arrive when they darn well feel like it. Second, when nothing's flying, the number of decoys you put out is irrelevant.

*F*act is, much of a waterfowler's time is spent waiting, and not every dawn brings skies full of flashing wings.

*T*hrough seasons of practice, the duck hunter has learned to preoccupy himself during the lean times instead of packing it in and possibly missing the hunt of his life.

A lull in the action means he can look for the guts to the $100 duck call dangling uselessly from his lanyard . . .

*O*r attempt to fix his broken-down outboard or shell-jammed gun.

*Y*et, truth be told, there are days when even a hardened waterfowler has trouble staying motivated.

hat's right: Wet and cold are the waterfowler's constant hunt-
g partners. Even when he's by himself, a cold or wet duck
unter is never truly alone.

In fact, with his hands stinging from sub-zero cold and his ear frozen solid, he's as likely to think *Hello, old friend* as he is *this really sucks*!

*E*very waterfowler knows that getting wet comes with the territory. And the water can come from anywhere. From above...

*F*rom below . . .

From the side . . .

rom your dog . . .

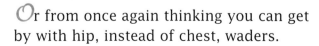

*F*rom one wrong step . . .

*O*r from once again thinking you can get by with hip, instead of chest, waders.

*I*n fact, sometimes it seems like water is coming from everywhere.

And sometimes it's true!

*H*unt waterfowl long enough and you'll spend as much time trying to keep water out as you will trying to bring ducks and geese in.

Of course, some hunters deserve to get wet. The trouble is, if he goes down, so will you.

ut who said life was fair, especially when it comes to leaky waders?

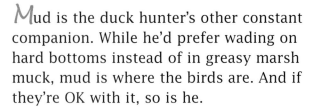

Mud is the duck hunter's other constant companion. While he'd prefer wading on hard bottoms instead of in greasy marsh muck, mud is where the birds are. And if they're OK with it, so is he.

*I*t's the unexpected adversities that truly test the waterfowlers resolve. So, although you might take an untimely spill getting out of the boat . . .

nly to be Rebel's love interest upon reaching shore, it helps to look on the bright side.

At least you didn't miss a REALLY EASY shot while a photographer was in the boat!

our trusty Lab didn't break when you had two honkers dead to rights, forcing you to pull off the shot.

And at least Rebel didn't roll in something disgusting before clasping onto your leg!

So, although your reed might stick now and then when the greenheads are circling, cheer up. You could be stuck listening to your buddy's guest flare every duck in sight.

You could look like a total rookie after finally being invited to a friend's exclusive duck blind.

You could be the best caller in the county and still have every duck you call in flare wildly away from your blind.

*Y*our partner could torpedo your morning hunt by showing you the easy way to unload a johnboat.

*I*n other words, everything's relative, and water-fowlers know that better than anyone. Still, it bears repeating. The next time you think about how much effort went into one tiny duck . . .

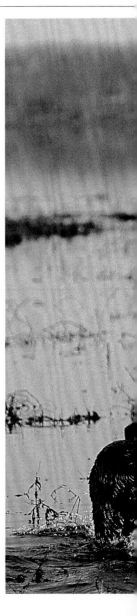

*R*emember: You could have been hunt-ing with these guys!

103

*I*f for some reason you've questioned your sanity lately— wondered WHY THE HECK AM I DOING THIS TO MYSELF?—and in a moment of weakness, wished you were somewhere else or could find something to crawl under . . .

*D*on't despair. It's not as bad as you think. You really aren't crazy. There is a reason why you go through all this misery!

*B*ecause waterfowling is fun! No kidding!

Some days the action's great, the coffee never tastes better, you shoot a banded bird, or get to sit in a really cool chair . . .

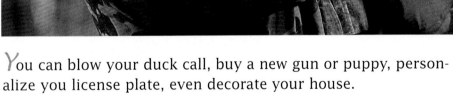

*Y*ou can blow your duck call, buy a new gun or puppy, personalize you license plate, even decorate your house.

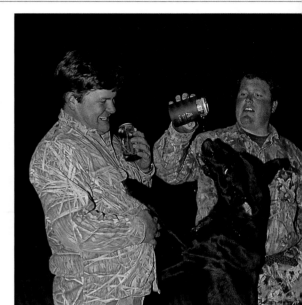

*B*est of all, you get to share great experiences with your closest friends. So fire up the Suburban and pile in. You're going to have a great time no matter what the weather brings, because you're in good company.

110

*J*ust don't get carried away with the bonding business. Misery may
love company, but this is ridiculous.